OXFORD

Andy Hopkins
and Joc Potter

Oxford Bookworms
Factfiles

OXFORD UNIVERSITY PRESS 1997

Oxford University Press, Great Clarendon Street,
Oxford OX2 6DP

Oxford   New York
Athens Auckland Bangkok Bogota Bombay
Buenos Aires Calcutta Cape Town
Dar es Salaam Delhi Florence Hong Kong
Istanbul Karachi Kuala Lumpur Madras
Madrid Melbourne Mexico City Nairobi Paris
Singapore Taipei Tokyo Toronto Warsaw

and associated companies in
Berlin Ibadan

OXFORD and OXFORD ENGLISH
are trade marks of Oxford University Press

ISBN 0 19 422847 9

© Oxford University Press

First published 1997

No unauthorized photocopying

All rights reserved. No part of this publication may be reproduced, stored in a retrieval system, or transmitted, in any form or by any means, electronic, mechanical, photocopying, recording or otherwise, without the prior written permission of Oxford University Press.

This book is sold subject to the condition that it shall not, by way of trade or otherwise, be lent, re-sold, hired out, or otherwise circulated without the publisher's prior consent in any form of binding or cover other than that in which it is published and without a similar condition including this condition being imposed on the subsequent purchaser.

Printed in Hong Kong

OXFORD BOOKWORMS
For a full list of titles in all the Oxford Bookworms series, please refer to the Oxford English catalogue.

Factfiles
Original readers giving varied and interesting information about a range of non-fiction topics. Titles available include:

Stage 1 (400 headwords)
Animals in Danger *Andy Hopkins and Joc Potter*
Flight *Michael Dean*
Kings and Queens of Britain *Tim Vicary*
London *John Escott*
New York *John Escott*

Stage 2 (700 headwords)
Football *Steve Flinders*
Forty Years of Pop *Steve Flinders*
Oxford *Andy Hopkins and Joc Potter*
Rainforests *Rowena Akinyemi*
Seasons and Celebrations *Jackie Maguire*
Under the Ground *Rosemary Border*

Stage 3 (1000 headwords)
Australia and New Zealand *Christine Lindop*
Recycling *Rosemary Border*
The Cinema *John Escott*

Black Series
Original stories and adaptations of classic and modern fiction.

Green Series
Adaptations of classic and modern stories for younger readers.

Oxford Bookworms Collection
Fiction by well known classic and modern authors. Texts are not abridged or simplified in any way.

ACKNOWLEDGEMENTS

The publishers would like to thank the following for their kind permission to reproduce photographs:

Cover photo of the Radcliffe Camera Pictor Uniphoto; Ancient Art and Architecture Collection p.5 Duke of Carmworth seizes bridle of Charles horse; British Motor Industry p.9 Morris Oxford 1920s; British Motor Museum p.9 William Morris – Lord Nuffield; Cogges Museum p.19 Cogges Manor Farm Museum, Main Kitchen; Collections/Anne Gordon p.3 The Old City Walls, Balliol and Merton Colleges; Collections/Keith Pritchard p.7 Oxford Canal; Collections p.9 Modern Rover Assembly Line;

Mary Evans Picture Library p.3 Canterbury Tales – Clerk of Oxford, p.7 Women Students in academic dress; Paul Freestone p.15 Punt on the River, May Morning Celebrations; Hulton Deutsch p.7 Tenniel Illustration of Alice, p.9 Morris Assembly Line; Rob Judges p.5 Martyrs Memorial, p.11 Tourists in Oxford, Traffic congestion in Cornmarket Street, p.16 Interior historic pub; Morrell's Brewery p.16 view of the entrance to the Brewery; Oxfam p.11 Oxfam's Famine Relief Work; Oxford Picture Library p.5 The Bodleian Library, p.15 The Covered Market, The University Boat Race; Pictor Uniphoto p.5 Sheldonian Theatre, p.19 Blenheim Palace, Cotswold Village Street; Tony Stone Images/Lorentz Gullachsen p.19 Shakespeare's Birthplace.

1 Oxford

Oxford is ninety kilometres from London – about an hour by car, bus or train – and only sixty-four kilometres from Heathrow Airport. The River Thames runs through Oxford, and the River Cherwell joins it there. The Thames then runs south-east towards London. The land is low, but there are hills to the west. Much of the city is old and very beautiful.

More than 110,000 people have their homes in Oxford. But in some months of the year there are a lot more people in the city; thousands of students come from other towns for parts of the year.

The city is an important centre for work, shopping and nightlife. But people from all over the world, and from different parts of Britain, come to Oxford to see the fine buildings, the museums, and the parks and gardens. Oxford is a very interesting city, and many visitors fall in love with it.

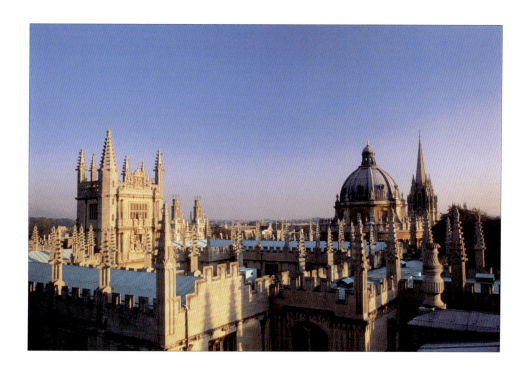

2 Early days

Oxford is not as old as some other English cities. London, York and Cambridge were already towns in Roman times. But by the tenth century Oxford was an important town.

At that time Oxford was a market town, on the river and with main roads running through it. There were walls around the town, and about five thousand people lived inside them.

The town got bigger in the twelfth century, when a lot of new houses were built. It was a rich business centre, selling cloth and wool. By the year 1200, there were new walls, three stone bridges across the river, a castle, sixteen churches and a palace. There were also the beginnings of a university.

Before that time, religious people went to the University of Paris to study; now they started to come to Oxford. Three colleges were built in the thirteenth century: University College, Balliol College and Merton College. They looked like religious buildings, and you can still see parts of these old buildings today. By the end of the thirteenth century there were 1500 students, and the university was already famous all over Europe.

New business for shopkeepers and other townspeople came from the larger number of university students, but there were also problems between the people of the town and those at the university. In 1209 some students killed a woman; angry townspeople then

The old city walls

killed two students, and many others moved away from Oxford. Some went to Cambridge and started the university there. In 1355 there was fighting in the streets for days, and sixty-two students died.

So there were problems, but Oxford was still getting bigger, and by the early fourteenth century it was a rich country town. Then a terrible illness called the Black Death killed nearly a third of the people there. Many who died were important businessmen, and the cloth industry did not bring as much money into the town as before.

The townspeople needed to find new work, and many more people began to work for students and the university. Students started to live in their houses and to eat the food they cooked. So the townspeople now needed the university more than in earlier times.

In his famous book *The Canterbury Tales*, the fourteenth-century writer Geoffrey Chaucer describes a poor student, The Clerk of Oxford. The Clerk is one of the first of many examples of Oxford students in English writing.

Merton College

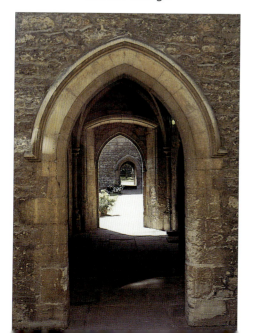

The Clerk of Oxford

3 Troubled times

Under the Protestant queen Elizabeth I (1558–1603), life in Oxford was easier than under her older, Catholic sister, 'Bloody Mary'; in Mary's time, three men were burned to death outside Balliol College for their religion. They are called the Oxford Martyrs.

In Elizabethan England there were still problems between Protestants and Catholics in Oxford, but the queen liked the city and visited it a number of times. It was fashionable for rich and important men to send their sons to the university; they used the town's facilities for eating, drinking and sports, and new colleges and university buildings were built.

The Bodleian Library, for example, opened in 1602. The library now has over 120 kilometres of books. Readers cannot take books out of the building, but they can find any British book there.

One of the Oxford Martyrs

The Bodleian Library

The Sheldonian Theatre was also built at this time. It was the work of Christopher Wren, who built St Paul's Cathedral in London. The university uses the Sheldonian on special days, but it is also open to visitors and for talks and concerts.

Oxford already had a cathedral (in Christ Church College) and was, by now, called a city. In the 1630s ten thousand people lived there; two thousand of these worked or studied at the university.

Between 1642 and 1646 there was a civil war in England; King Charles I's soldiers were fighting Oliver Cromwell's. Charles and his soldiers moved to Oxford. The king lived in one of the colleges, because most people at the university were on his side. Colleges also gave him their gold and silver. Important people from the city who were against the king went away until the war ended. There was fighting all around Oxford, and in the end Cromwell's soldiers controlled the city. The king got away, but in 1649 they cut off his head.

The Sheldonian Theatre

Charles I is taken prisoner

4 Out of the past

Some of Oxford's finest buildings are from the eighteenth century. The Radcliffe Camera, the first round library, was built for science books. The Clarendon Building was the home of the University Press which printed, and still prints, books for the university. The front of Queen's College was also built at this time.

Shopkeepers were doing well, and business with other parts of the country was easier after the Oxford Canal opened in 1790. Boats carried in things that were made in the factories of London and the towns to the north. Then, in 1844, the railway arrived in the city. After that even poorer people could travel to and from Oxford more easily.

The Oxford Canal

From the late eighteenth and nineteenth centuries, the city was cleaner, the roads were wider, and there was better street lighting. Oxford started to look like a modern city. A lot of cheaper houses were built in East Oxford and Jericho, mainly for people who worked for the university, the University Press, the railways, and other large businesses. More expensive houses in North Oxford were for richer people – heads of colleges and rich businessmen. Before this time, heads of colleges did not marry; they lived in their colleges. But in the nineteenth century more and more university teachers began to live outside their colleges.

By now the university was also more modern; religion was less important than before, and it was teaching more science. In 1879 the first two of four women's colleges opened. But there were no university degrees for women at that time. The first woman got her

Women students in 1879

Alice

degree in 1920. There were no colleges for men and women together until 1974.

All Oxford University students belong to a college. Many of them live and have classes there. Each college has its own facilities. Twenty-two British prime ministers (Margaret Thatcher, for example) studied at the university; many other famous people from around the world (like President Clinton of the United States and Prince Naruhito of Japan) were also students there. Writers like Graham Greene, Aldous Huxley and Oscar Wilde; actors like Richard Burton; scientists like Edmund Hailey … there is no end to the names of famous students.

Many writers were at Oxford as students and then moved away. Others, like Charles Dodgson, stayed to teach and write. Dodgson used the name Lewis Carroll and his most famous book is called *Alice's Adventures in Wonderland* (1865).

5 Oxford cars

One man who played a very important part in the history of Oxford was William Morris.

Morris lived in Oxford when he was a child and his first job, when he was fourteen, was mending bicycles. He also enjoyed racing them in his free time. Then, in 1893, Morris started buying bicycle parts and making the machines himself. He opened a shop in the city centre to sell them.

He liked cars too, and he made his first car in 1913. Later he opened a car factory in Cowley, in the south-east of Oxford. In the first year he built nearly four hundred Morris Oxfords. The business got bigger and bigger, and by the end of the 1920s Morris was building 100,000 cars a year. By 1938, 10,000 people worked in the factories.

In the 1920s Morris decided to change from wood and metal to steel for his cars. He had talks with an American steel company, and they also started a business in Oxford.

After the Second World War, Morris's company joined with others and changed its name a

Morris – 1930

Rover today

number of times. The Morris Minor, the little Mini and many other famous cars came from the Cowley factory. In the early 1970s more than 26,000 people worked in the city's car industry, making thousands of cars each week.

Cars are still made in Oxford under the name of Rover. The business is not as important to Oxford as before, but in his time William Morris helped to make Oxford a modern city.

Morris worked until the age of eighty-three. He was very rich, but he had no children and he gave a lot of money to hospitals and for research. He also used his money to open a new Oxford college, Nuffield College. In all, he gave away about £30 million. William Morris died in 1963.

An early Morris

William Morris

6 The modern city

The largest industrial company in the 1830s, when it moved to its new building in Walton Street, was Oxford University Press. The Press is still important in the world of books, and it is internationally famous. It has offices in a large number of countries and publishes books in many languages. Other publishers, like Heinemann Educational Books, Nuffield Press and Blackwell's, also have their main offices in Oxford.

Many people work in the city's hospitals, and in scientific research. There are a lot of new but important businesses in the Oxford Science Park.

Oxfam is a charity that started in Oxford during the Second World War to help people in Greece. These people were dying because food could not get to them. After the war the charity decided to help other people around the world who were

Printing in 1850

hungry or homeless. At first they sent food, clothes and other useful things to foreign countries. Now they try to help the poor (in more than seventy countries) to help themselves. In Britain nearly all of Oxfam's money (about £80 million a year) comes from ordinary British people and from the charity's shops. Many of the people who work for Oxfam give their time free.

Nearly two million people visit Oxford each year, and forty per cent of these are from other countries. Visitors to the city need hotels, food and drink, and other facilities, so a lot of people work in the tourist industry.

Like other big cities, Oxford has problems with traffic and the shopping streets are often very crowded. But these show that the city is alive – and working.

Oxfam at work

Tourists in Broad Street

Traffic in Cornmarket Street

7 Oxford by day

Oxford is a beautiful city by day. The university gardens and the parks and fields around the river make the centre of Oxford a surprisingly green place. In good weather, visitors also love walking through the narrow old streets between the university buildings, and around the Botanic Garden (from 1621), the oldest in Britain.

Many people travel around the city by bicycle. At any one time there are about twenty thousand bicycles on the streets. Another way to see Oxford is from one of the many open-top buses. But if you want to get away from streets and traffic, you can enjoy the river from a punt. In the old days people used these boats to carry passengers and animals down the river, but now students and tourists use them.

Oxford has some of Britain's finest museums. There is the Ashmolean, the home of the university's works of art and the oldest museum in the world that is open to everyone; the Museum of the History of Science; the University Museum, and the Museum of Modern Art. The Pitt-Rivers Museum holds over a million interesting things which travellers in foreign countries sent back to Oxford in the eighteenth and nineteenth centuries. To learn how Oxford has changed over the centuries, you can visit the Museum of Oxford or The Oxford Story. They tell the story of the city using pictures, sounds and even smells from different times in the past.

Punts

The Covered Market in the centre of the city is an old food market that was built in 1774. Today it sells meat, fish, vegetables, flowers, and other things. There is also a much newer open market place in Gloucester Green, near the bus station.

The old and the new are side by side in Oxford. You can visit modern shopping centres or the smaller shops in the old streets. And if you are looking for books, Oxford is the place to come.

Blackwell's is the largest bookseller. The family's first shop opened in 1879, and they now have nine bookshops in the city. The Norrington Room, in the main shop, holds more books than any other single room in a bookshop in the world.

Then there are sports. You can play them – or you can watch. The city's football clubs are Oxford United and Oxford City, and a lot of people go to their home matches.

The Covered Market

8 Special days

Very early on May Morning, May 1st, hundreds of people wait in the street outside Magdalen College, and at six o'clock there is singing from the top of the building. The rest of the morning is a street party. People dance, talk, drink and enjoy themselves. A few students make the dangerous jump from Magdalen Bridge into the river below.

St Giles' Fair is in early September. It started centuries ago. People came into the city to buy and sell, eat and drink, and play sports. A hundred years ago it was even fashionable to show strange animals and people at the fair.

May 1st

Oxford

The Boat Race takes place on the Thames in London every year. It is a race between the universities of Oxford (in dark blue) and Cambridge (in light blue). People watch from the bridges or the sides of the river, and many more watch it on television.

Eights Week is a week of boat races on the River Cherwell in Oxford. This time the races are between the different colleges. The river is narrow, so boats race one behind the other and try to touch the boat in front.

Eights Week

9 Oxford by night

People were already making beer in Oxford seven hundred years ago, and by the late fourteenth century there were thirty-two brewers making beer. In more modern times, one of the most important brewers is Morrell's. Morrell's started making beer in 1792; today the company is still in the same building, and the same family controls it.

You can enjoy Oxford's beers in the very large number of pubs in and around the city. Some pubs are on the busy central streets and squares; others are beside the river or out in the quiet of the country. There are pubs with live music and pubs with popular games.

Many pubs sell food, but if you prefer to eat in a restaurant, you can choose cheap or expensive food from Britain, Italy, China, India and other parts of the world.

There are a number of cinemas in Oxford and two main theatres. The Oxford Playhouse and the Apollo Theatre have theatre, music and dance. The Old Fire Station also has a small theatre, and music in the bar. And, of course, Oxford also has late night live music and discos.

Morrell's Brewery

An Oxford pub

10 Around Oxford

Oxford is a good centre for visits to the towns and villages in the country around it.

One of the first places to visit is the small country town of Woodstock, about thirteen kilometres away. Most visitors to Woodstock go to Blenheim Palace, the eighteenth century home of the Dukes of Marlborough, and the place where Winston Churchill was born. You can go inside the palace to look at fine old pictures and furniture in beautiful rooms; the Long Library, fifty-five metres from end to end, is one of the longest rooms in an English family home.

You can walk in the palace gardens and the park. The park is very large, so there is a small train that travels across part of it. You can take a boat out on the water, eat, drink, shop and play.

Blenheim Palace

A Cotswold village

To the west of Oxford are the Cotswold hills with their villages and small towns of yellow-grey stone. On Burford's fine high street you can see houses that were built, long ago, with money from wool and from the many travellers who came through the town. Near Burford is the Cotswold Wildlife Park, which keeps animals, fish and birds.

Other good examples of beautiful Cotswold towns and villages are Chipping Campden (from where you can walk 145 kilometres along the Cotswold Way to the historic city of Bath) and Bourton-on-the-Water, on the River Windrush. Both of these get thousands of visitors in the summer months.

At Cogges Manor Farm Museum, near the town of Witney, you can watch people using kitchens, farm machines and animals in the ways that they used them a hundred years ago. On different summer weekends, people from the farm show visitors how to make bread, cover books or cut the wool from sheep. There is sometimes singing and dancing there too.

Oxford

Stratford-upon-Avon (forty-eight kilometres away) is famous as the place where William Shakespeare was born. People from all over the world go there to look at his house, his school and his wife's home. They also visit the theatres in Stratford to see works by Shakespeare and by other important writers. Shakespeare often stayed the night in Oxford when he was travelling from Stratford to London.

Leaving Oxford by the railway towards London, the first stop is at Didcot, which is famous for its Railway Centre. There you can look at old trains, and sometimes it is possible to ride on them.

Down the Thames, south of Oxford, are places like Abingdon, Dorchester and Wallingford, which are all older than Oxford. These and many other places make Oxford an interesting city to travel from.

A visitor study shows that eighty per cent of visitors prefer Oxford to other historic British towns. They do not like the traffic or the crowds, but they do like the buildings, the history and the shops. For most people Oxford is a very interesting place.

Cogges Manor Farm Museum

Shakespeare's birthplace, Stratford

Exercises

A Checking your understanding

Pages 1–3 *Are these sentences true (T) or false (F)?*
1 Oxford is south of London.
2 It is the oldest city in Britain.
3 Parts of the university are more than 700 years old.
4 The townspeople did not always like the university students.

Pages 4–7 *Who ...*
1 ... built the Sheldonian Theatre?
2 ... lost his head?
3 ... lived in North Oxford?
4 ... could not get a degree until this century?

Pages 8–11 *Write answers to these questions.*
1 Why is Cowley a famous part of Oxford?
2 What does Oxford University Press do?
3 How does Oxfam get money to give away?
4 How many foreign visitors come to Oxford each year?

Pages 12–15 *Find answers to these questions.*
1 How can you travel on the river?
2 Where can you learn more about the story of Oxford?
3 Which Oxford bookshop has got most books?
4 Why do people stand outside Magdalen College on May 1st?

Pages 16–19 *What ...*
1 ... does Morrell's make?
2 ... is the Oxford Playhouse?
3 ... is the name of the Duke of Marlborough's home?
4 ... can you see at the Cotswold Wildlife Park?

B Working with language

1 *Complete these sentences with information from the book.*

   1 In the 12th century Oxford was a rich town because …
   2 In the 13th century two students were killed, so …
   3 King Charles I moved to Oxford because …
   4 After the Oxford Canal opened in 1790, …

2 *Put these sentences about William Morris in the right order. Then check your order with pages 8–9.*
   1 He used steel to make cars.
   2 He started selling bicycles.
   3 The company name changed to Rover.
   4 He mended bicycles.
   5 He made cars from wood and metal.

C Activities

1 You are going to spend three days in and around Oxford. Plan your visit. What are you going to do each day? Then write a paragraph about your plans.

2 Your holiday in Oxford is at an end. Describe one of the days that you spent there.

D Project work

1 Find more information about one of these famous people, and write about him.
   Geoffrey Chaucer   Oliver Cromwell   Winston Churchill

2 Look for information about a famous person who was born in your town, or who visited it. Write his or her story.

Glossary

art things like pictures that people think are beautiful

beer an alcoholic drink

cathedral a big, important church

century one hundred years; the 13th century starts in the year 1200

cloth something that you use to make clothes, cover furniture, etc.

college a place, often part of a university, where people learn after they leave school

company a business

concert music that a group of people play or sing to other people

degree the paper that shows you did well at university

facility something that you can use when you want to, e.g. sports facilities

industry work that uses people and machines to make things, often in a factory

museum a building where there are beautiful, old and interesting things for people to look at

press a business that prints books

print put letters and pictures on to paper, using a machine

publish print a book and sell it

race something that you win if you are the fastest

religion feelings about life and death that come from knowing God

research deep study to find new information

science the study of the ways in which the world works

steel a strong, hard metal

study spend time learning about something

war a time of fighting between countries; a civil war is a war between two groups from the same country

wool soft hair from a sheep